NEW MAGIC VALLEY FUN TOWN

ALSO BY DANIEL MACIVOR

Try: Communion, Was Spring, Small Things
One Voice: House and Here Lies Henry
Never Swim Alone & This Is a Play
See Bob Run & Wild Abandon
This Is What Happens Next
I Still Love You: Five Plays
Who Killed Spalding Gray?
The Soldier Dreams
The Best Brothers
Marion Bridge
Arigato, Tokyo
His Greatness
How It Works
You Are Here
Cul-de-sac
I, Animal
Monster
In On It
Bingo!

NEW MAGIC VALLEY FUN TOWN

DANIEL MACIVOR

PLAYWRIGHTS CANADA PRESS
TORONTO

Library and Archives Canada Cataloguing in Publication
Title: New magic valley fun town / Daniel MacIvor.
Names: MacIvor, Daniel, 1962- author.
Description: A play.
Identifiers: Canadiana (print) 20200370650 | Canadiana (ebook) 20200370693 | ISBN 9780369101334 (softcover) | ISBN 9780369101341 (PDF) | ISBN 9780369101358 (EPUB) | ISBN 9780369101365 (Kindle)
Classification: LCC PS8575.I86 N49 2020 | DDC C812/.54—dc23

Playwrights Canada Press operates on Mississaugas of the Credit, Wendat, Anishinaabe, Métis, and Haudenosaunee land. It always was and always will be Indigenous land.

We acknowledge the financial support of the Canada Council for the Arts—which last year invested $153 million to bring the arts to Canadians throughout the country—the Ontario Arts Council (OAC), Ontario Creates, and the Government of Canada for our publishing activities.

Canada Council for the Arts | Conseil des arts du Canada

ONTARIO ARTS COUNCIL
CONSEIL DES ARTS DE L'ONTARIO
an Ontario government agency
un organisme du gouvernement de l'Ontario

Canada

ONTARIO CREATES | ONTARIO CRÉATIF

For Buster and Joseph Neil

FOREWORD

CAROLINE GILLIS

I'm writing these notes at the end of October 2020 and it's a fascinating time to be doing so. I just finished isolating after facing a possible COVID-19 exposure. Luckily, it was a false alarm. In a non-pandemic world, we would be performing *New Magic Valley Fun Town* in Calgary right now, but the current state of affairs led to the cancellation of three scheduled productions of the show.

I only heard the phrase "grief is the price of love" a couple of years ago and I was startled by its acuity. Daniel's play, although not a biography of his life, is in many ways an ode to his brother. Joe passed away a few months after we finished our run of the show in Halifax. This summer I lost my brother Steve during the pandemic, so I have been thinking a lot about and experiencing grief. And collectively as a global community we are apparently suffering from a kind of grief as well for the loss of *life as we know it.*

Daniel once said to me that writing must cost you something. He examines his grief and pain through his work to make sense of it. And I have witnessed this as a frequent performer in his plays, including *New Magic Valley Fun Town*, a play that he has described as starting out as a slapstick comedy and ending with the recitation of a poem.

Dougie and Cheryl, along with their daughter Sandy, await the arrival of Dougie's childhood friend Allen. In rehearsal we talked a lot about the secrets that these flawed and conflicted characters carry, from simple white lies to the devastation of childhood trauma. Trauma that reverberates through their own corrupted attempts at love and *life as they knew it.*

As a fellow Cape Bretoner both to the playwright and the characters, I know they are a stoic people whose sense of humour often belies the great sense of love they hold for their family and friends. Not being able to hug in these isolating times may not necessarily be a bad thing for a fourth-generation Scottish immigrant trying to protect herself from her feelings. It's best not to talk about it. Let it blow over. Time heals all wounds.

Like the characters in the play, we have a tendency to blur our pain with whatever denial works for us. Too much alcohol, overeating, or Cheryl's favourite, *keeping busy*. We build up layers of insulation to numb ourselves to our grief. There is a depth of love behind the characters of *New Magic Valley Fun Town* that underlies their unspoken motivations. They keep coming back to each other but can't seem to verbalize why. When at a certain point Dougie chokes out the words "I love you," it is both devastating and freeing. Daniel is at the top of his game here as a playwright. Great theatre pierces through the layers we have built up as humans and audience members and becomes a catalyst for change.

My first word as a child was "Stevie." Now when I say out loud, "My brother Steve died . . . " it chokes me up as the grief I am feeling makes a rush to my throat to escape. I can't control it. Like good writing, it costs. Grief is the price of love.

As Sandy and Dougie choke out the words of her poem together at the end of the play, we can see that true healing may actually begin.

I carry you home,
now an ember in the ash.
Glowing goodness.
We will see now how simple,
how good
how true.

I carry you with me.

Caroline Gillis grew up in Cape Breton and currently resides in Toronto, where she has been an actor for over thirty years. She has appeared in theatres across Canada, from the Belfry in Victoria to the Neptune in Halifax. She has had a long-term working relationship with Daniel MacIvor, first appearing in See Bob Run *in 1987 and most recently performing in* New Magic Valley Fun Town. *Others include* Communion, A Beautiful View, *and* Marion Bridge. *She narrated the audiobook* Into That Fire *for Penguin Random House and recently appeared in* Mrs. America *(FX/Hulu). Caroline is the author of her own play* Caveman Rainbow *and has an MA in Theatre Studies from the University of Guelph.*

New Magic Valley Fun Town was first produced by Prairie Theatre Exchange and Tarragon Theatre at Prairie Theatre Exchange, Winnipeg, from January 25 to February 10, 2019, with the following cast and creative team:

Cheryl: Caroline Gillis
Sandy: Stephanie MacDonald
Dougie: Daniel MacIvor
Allen: Andrew Moodie

Director: Richard Rose
Assistant Director: Audrey Dwyer
Set Design: Brian Perchaluk
Costume Design: Brenda McLean
Lighting Design: Kimberly Purtell
Sound Design: Don Benedictson
Choreographer: Brenda Gorlick
Stage Manager: Marinda de Beer
Assistant Stage Manager: Robin Munro

CHARACTERS

Dougie: fifties, white, thin, high-energy, bald to thinning hair, ill but currently rallying.

Cheryl: fifties, white, good-natured but pugnacious, practising Catholic, formerly married to Dougie.

Sandy: thirties, white, sensual, somewhat lost, highly intelligent, daughter of Dougie and Cheryl.

Allen: fifties, Black, kind but troubled, academic, old childhood friend of Dougie and Cheryl.

SETTING

Near Sydney, Cape Breton, outside the city limits.

The set is a cross-section of Dougie's trailer that exposes the length of the trailer. There's a living room/kitchen and a long hallway that leads off to two bedrooms and a bathroom. The entrance from outside is into the kitchen area. In the kitchen is a small window and in the living room a larger window, both of which look out onto the front deck that Dougie has built himself. In the living room is a sofa, recliner, coffee table and side table with a boom box.

Downstage of the trailer is an acting area that represents an area outside and "behind" the trailer. Here and in the living room are where the final scene will occur.

SCENE 1

The trailer is pristine. Scrubbed and vacuumed. There is a sense that even at the worst of times an OCD *neatness prevails. Surfaces are not cluttered but there are a few knick-knacks and half a dozen framed photographs. Some sports memorabilia on the walls—New York Yankees, Toronto Maple Leafs. A closed laptop sits on the kitchen counter, plugged in and charging.*

Light shift.

A car approaches. A door slams, the trunk slams. Soon DOUGIE *comes into view through the windows and up the steps to the deck.* DOUGIE *struggles with his key in the lock. His hands and arms are full—three or four plastic grocery bags filled with snack foods and soda pop, two cases of beer, paper bags from the liquor store, one holding wine and one holding hard liquor. Along with all of this he holds a large Tim's takeout coffee in one hand. He wears pressed work pants and a plaid shirt neatly tucked in.*

Even though DOUGIE *is hidden behind this pile of party supplies we can tell he is agitated. He slowly makes his way into the trailer and manages to get through the door without dropping anything. Before stepping into the trailer properly he kicks off his runners on a mat at the door. This is an impressive balancing act. He makes an effort to keep the shoes on the mat, even though this makes his job that much more difficult. He succeeds. Now deshoed he makes his way toward the kitchen counter, where he carefully sets down his load. The beer and alcohol are safe, the plastic bags neatly beside them. He takes a breath. He takes a sip of coffee. He notices that his shoes are not perfectly lined up on the mat. As he moves to the mat to correct this he knocks the bag of wine off the counter and it falls to the floor with a smash.*

DOUGIE
NO!

Wine seeps out of the bag all over the kitchen floor. DOUGIE *tries to scoop up the bag, and wine now pours out.*

No no no no no no no no no no no no.

DOUGIE *manages to get the bag into the sink. He has made a mess on the floor.*

No no no no.

DOUGIE *pulls a paper towel from the roll on the counter. It is the last towel left.*

Goddamn goddamn goddamn goddamn.

DOUGIE *grabs tea towels hanging from the stove to mop up the liquid.*

No no no no.

As he moves around the room we notice that he has some discomfort getting down or standing up.

Fuckers fuckers fuckers.

He wipes up most of the spill.

Goddamn goddamn goddamn.

Now finished, he rises. He picks up his coffee to have a sip. It slips from his hand and explodes on the floor.

NO!

He explodes.

Fuckers!

He picks up one of his shoes and yells at it.

Fuckers!

He throws his shoe at the door.

Fuckers!

He collapses into a chair, his head in his hands.

No no no no no no no no no no no no no no no no no.

DOUGIE *gets himself together. He takes a couple of deep breaths. He goes to his prominently displayed boom box and puts on a nearby CD. An upbeat song from his high school days, maybe Steve Winwood's "Higher Love." He dances a bit. He lines up his shoes carefully on the mat. He mops up some of the spill and drops the coffee cup and lid in the sink. Rather than finish cleaning up, he locks the door so no one will enter and walk through the mess. He goes into the bathroom. The music continues.*

After a few moments CHERYL *is at the door.*

CHERYL
Dougie?
Dougie! The door's locked!
For God's sake . . .

CHERYL *pushes the small window in the door open and moves the screen over. She snakes her arm through the opening and unlocks the door. She enters. She is dressed in Winners casual, as she is eventually on her way to Mass. She is carrying a bag from the grocery store containing a huge package of paper towels.* CHERYL *turns off the music.*

Dougie?

She hears the bathtub running. She takes off her shoes and places them on the mat.

Are you having your sponge bath?
Are you having your sponge bath?
Dougie!

CHERYL *makes her way back into the kitchen.*

What was the door locked for?

CHERYL *walks through the wet spot on the floor.*

What in God's green—?

CHERYL *goes to the sink.*

For the love of—
Dougie?
What's this mess?

She sees the bag with broken wine bottles and sopping tea towels in the sink. She approaches the bathroom door.

Dougie?

DOUGIE
(off) Jesus, Cheryl! You scared the shit out of me.

CHERYL
What's this mess?

DOUGIE
(off) There weren't any paper towels!

CHERYL
I walked through it!

DOUGIE
(off) That's why I had the door locked so you wouldn't traipse it everywhere.

CHERYL
That's going to be sticky as sin.

DOUGIE
(off) There weren't any paper towels!

CHERYL
(re: mess in sink) Who are you buying wine for?

CHERYL opens up the package of paper towels and begins sopping up the damp spots on the floor.

(off to DOUGIE) Sandy's not drinking. I can't imagine Charky drinks wine. All he ever drank was beer and rum from what I remember.
Don't be buying wine for Sandy. She might not even come tonight.

DOUGIE
(off) Sandy's coming.

CHERYL
I don't know, she's in a mood. Quiet and mean. The meanest mean, the quiet kind. The only thing she said to me all afternoon is, "Why do you even bother dying your hair anymore?"

As CHERYL continues speaking she stops cleaning the floor and stealthily opens a cupboard that has one shelf mostly filled with medications. Keeping an ear on the bathroom she finds a particular bottle and counts how many pills are in it. Once done she looks through the rest of the medications until she hears DOUGIE coming.

Buddy Walsh asked how you were doing. Him and Clare were up at Tim's. Tim's at Grand Lake, not at the mall. I think they must be living out the cottage full time now.

DOUGIE
(off) What were you doing out in Grand Lake?

CHERYL
I was taking Brenda for her coffee. She likes the Grand Lake Tim's better. She says they put nutmeg in the mall's Tim's coffee because nutmeg is addictive. Did you ever hear that?

DOUGIE
(off) Ridiculous!

CHERYL
Tim's are all the same to me, tea is tea. Except that steeped tea—I tried their steeped tea but I'd rather just put milk in with the bag. That steeped tea tastes like something you'd make camping.

The water shuts off in the bathroom.

Are you done your sponge bath?

DOUGIE
(off) Yes, Cheryl.
Could you please not call it a sponge bath?

CHERYL
What do you want me to call it?

DOUGIE
(off) Just call it a bath!

CHERYL
Okay.
Are you doing up your dressing? Do you need a hand?
Are you doing up your dressing?

DOUGIE
(off) Yes.

CHERYL
Do you need a—

DOUGIE
(off) No, Cheryl.

CHERYL

Buddy Walsh asked after you. He's always so nice. Haven't had a mayor like Buddy Walsh around here in a while. Working for the people, not just doing favours for his friends.
He was good to us in the office and you too, all the boys in the yard, all the staff. He knew all of our names. This new mayor though, what a rig, God. Nothing but a politician. No humanity.

DOUGIE

(off) Who cares.

CHERYL

Certainly not our best and brightest called to that line of work anymore. Think back to when we were kids, the Kennedys and all that in those days. It was regal or . . . higher than regular life.

DOUGIE

(off) What are you talking about the Kennedys for?

CHERYL

Camelot and Jackie O.

DOUGIE

(off) The Kennedys were no saints.

CHERYL

They were heroic. Buddy Walsh was too. He saved those kids from that forest fire. Imagine this rig running into a forest fire? Brenda says he's building a house out on the point for the girlfriend. And nobody's batting an eye. Not even his wife. I feel so bad for her. That's what happens you marry a politician. Getting away with murder now all of them.
Or I don't know, maybe they always did but we didn't know.
Now we know.
I think I'd rather not know to tell you the truth.

She hears the bathroom door open. She quickly closes the cupboard and pretends to be looking through the bags on the counter. DOUGIE *comes out of the bathroom in a ratty old bathrobe, work socks and boxer shorts.*

DOUGIE
Cheryl . . . ?

CHERYL
Well I know what I'm getting you for Christmas.

DOUGIE
What?

CHERYL
A new bathrobe.
Who are you buying wine for?

DOUGIE
Does it smell like smoke in here?

CHERYL
Yes.

DOUGIE
Jesus, I aired the place out for two days.

CHERYL
Fifteen years takes longer than two days to get rid of.

DOUGIE
What am I going to do?

DOUGIE *opens the front door and fans at it, trying to air the place out further.*

CHERYL
Maybe Charky still smokes.

DOUGIE
Oh my God, Cheryl, Charky wouldn't still smoke.

CHERYL
He might.

DOUGIE
He's a runner.

CHERYL
Oh he's not a runner.

DOUGIE
Did you not see his Facebook?

CHERYL
There was pictures of him in a race. That doesn't mean anything. Facebook's all lies.

DOUGIE
Charky's not a liar.

CHERYL
Who knows what he is. You haven't seen him in thirty-five years.

DOUGIE
No. He was here summer that time.

CHERYL
Oh God, thirty years then.

DOUGIE
Cheryl, we known each other since we were this high.

CHERYL
I know. I knew him too.

DOUGIE
You know him to be a liar? 'Cause I never did.

CHERYL
No.

DOUGIE
So?

CHERYL
All right.
Still doesn't mean he's a runner.

DOUGIE
Cheryl, let it go.

> DOUGIE *closes the door. He notices the cupboard door is slightly ajar and closes it.*

What did you say when Buddy Walsh asked how I was doing?

CHERYL
I told him you were doing good.

DOUGIE
Yeah. And how many stitches I had and which prescriptions I'm on and the astrological sign of my oncologist.

CHERYL
I don't talk about you like that.

DOUGIE
Oh you talk about me like that. You talk about me like that to Brenda, I heard you.

CHERYL
I can talk to my sister like that. I can talk to family like that.

DOUGIE
She's not my family.

CHERYL
Oh for God's sake.
What happened here with the mess?

DOUGIE
Nothing.

CHERYL
Did you get mad and do that on purpose?

DOUGIE
God, Cheryl, no.
I asked you to pick up paper towels.

CHERYL
And I did.

DOUGIE
Two days ago.

CHERYL
I got 'em. They're here. It's clean.

DOUGIE
I'm just saying I needed them before.

CHERYL
They're here now.

DOUGIE
If you don't want to do something just tell me you don't want to do it.

CHERYL
I didn't not want to do it. I didn't get the chance till now.

DOUGIE
I would have done it myself but you said you were doing it.

CHERYL
I did it. It's done. It's all cleaned up. You're welcome.

DOUGIE
I just want things to be nice that's all.

CHERYL
Show me your dressing.

DOUGIE
God . . .

> DOUGIE *opens his bathrobe and shows her the bandaging on his back covering an operation wound.* CHERYL *inspects it carefully.*

Is it stuck down all the way in the back?

CHERYL
You did good.

DOUGIE
I'm not going back to that petri dish hospital for another fucking infection.

CHERYL
You put some weight on.

DOUGIE
Oh thank you very much, Cheryl.

CHERYL
That's good!

> DOUGIE *spies something out the window.*

DOUGIE
Fucking kids.

> *He dashes to the door and yells out the screen.*

Get off the lawn!

CHERYL
Dougie, don't!

> DOUGIE *dashes to the window to watch unseen.*

For God's sake, Dougie . . .

> CHERYL *grabs a litre of soda pop from the counter. She heads out the door and off.*

DOUGIE
Cheryl!

CHERYL
(stepping out of view) Here, fellas, don't mind the old grouch, have some pop!

DOUGIE
(to himself) Have some pop?

CHERYL re-enters the trailer.

Have some pop?

CHERYL
Are you out of you mind altogether, Dougie? Don't go making enemies of teenagers.

DOUGIE
They're always out there smoking pot.

CHERYL
It's just vaping.

DOUGIE
What do you think they're vaping? Bubble gum?

CHERYL
Maybe.
That's not even your property

DOUGIE
I mow it.

CHERYL goes to the window.

CHERYL
There they go, happy as clams with their pop.

DOUGIE goes to the cupboard and opens it elaborately. He studies the bottles there a moment then takes one out and shakes it, getting CHERYL's attention.

DOUGIE
Were you snooping, Cheryl?

CHERYL
No.

DOUGIE
Don't snoop, Cheryl.

CHERYL
Are you taking your pain pills?

DOUGIE
Not at the moment.

CHERYL
Have you been taking them?

DOUGIE
You tell me, you're the snoop.

CHERYL
They help the healing.

DOUGIE
I do not like how they make me feel.

CHERYL
But—

DOUGIE
Leave it.

After a moment.

CHERYL
Was the mall busy? Saturday's crazy up there.

DOUGIE
Oh good, you put the macaroni and cheese in the fridge already did you?

CHERYL
Oh God.

DOUGIE
Oh dear, you didn't forget it.

CHERYL
Shit.

DOUGIE
Did it slip your mind?

CHERYL
Yes. I'm sorry.

DOUGIE
I knew you'd forget it.

CHERYL
I'll go back.

DOUGIE
Sandy's bringing it.

CHERYL
You knew I forgot it?

DOUGIE
I know you well, Cheryl.

CHERYL
Sandy told you she's bringing it?

DOUGIE
Yeah.

CHERYL
So you knew I forgot it?

DOUGIE
Yeah.

CHERYL
But you asked me where it was anyway?

DOUGIE
I knew you'd forget it.

CHERYL
So that's just pretty much just straight out lying, you know that right?

DOUGIE
What's lying?

CHERYL
Knowing I forgot it and asking me if I did.

DOUGIE
That's not lying.

CHERYL
What is it then?

DOUGIE
Proving a point.

CHERYL
And what's your point?

DOUGIE
How well I know you, Cheryl.

CHERYL
Oh, Dougie, you'd be surprised. There are worlds inside me you could never imagine.

DOUGIE
Is that so?

CHERYL
You never know what I might do next. This weekend I'm going antique hunting with Brenda.

DOUGIE
Antique hunting? Well well, look at you, next thing you'll be going on a cruise.

CHERYL
Oh God, a cruise, no thank you, a floating septic tank.

DOUGIE
(laughing) Floating septic tank, that's about the size of it.

We hear a car approaching. DOUGIE *goes to the window.*

CHERYL
Who are you buying wine for?

DOUGIE
Why are you asking me that?

CHERYL
Sandy's not drinking.

DOUGIE
That's not what she told me.

CHERYL
She can't drink on that new medication.

DOUGIE
As far as I know she stopped taking the medication.

CHERYL
No.
When?

DOUGIE
Last week maybe.

CHERYL
Last week?

DOUGIE
Oh God, I don't know, ask her yourself.

We hear a car pulling in.

CHERYL
She's a sneaky one she is.

DOUGIE
The only problem you two have is you're too much alike.

CHERYL
(under her breath) Who's alike?

DOUGIE
What?

CHERYL
Go get dressed.

DOUGIE
(mocking) Go get dressed.

DOUGIE *exits to his bedroom to change.*

CHERYL *watches briefly after* DOUGIE *then picks up one of the cases of beer. She puts her shoes on, waiting at the door.*

SANDY *appears at the door carrying a casserole dish. She is wearing pyjamas and slippers.*

CHERYL
Clear the way.

SANDY
What are you doing?

CHERYL
Clear the way.

As CHERYL *quickly darts out:*

SANDY
What are you doing?

CHERYL
He's getting changed.

SANDY
Where are you going with that?

CHERYL
One sec.

CHERYL is gone.

SANDY enters and looks down the hall for DOUGIE and sees that he is out of sight. She puts the casserole dish down on the counter. She goes to the cupboard and checks the same bottle of pills that CHERYL checked earlier. She puts them back. She looks at the other medications, then the broken bottles and wet tea towels in the sink. CHERYL returns.

SANDY
Where did you go with that?

CHERYL
Oh my God your father doesn't need all this beer. I put it in the trunk of my car. If it turns out it's needed, fine it's there. My bet is he won't even notice it's gone. I don't know if Charky even drinks anymore. Apparently he's a runner.
Take off your shoes.

SANDY
They're slippers.

CHERYL
They've been outside? Take them off.

SANDY takes them off.

On the mat.

SANDY complies.

Help me with this.

SANDY
What happened with the stuff in the sink?

CHERYL
Who knows.

CHERYL begins putting the beer in the refrigerator. SANDY lies on the sofa checking social media.

SANDY
Did he do it on purpose?

CHERYL
No.

SANDY
Did you make him mad?

CHERYL
No, Sandy.
He's fine tonight.
And let's keep it that way.

SANDY
"Me" let's keep it that way?

CHERYL
Did I say you? I didn't say you.

SANDY
Good then.

CHERYL
How's that new medication working out for you?

SANDY
Good.

CHERYL
Good.

SANDY
Really good.

CHERYL
Good.

CHERYL *puts the snacks and liquor away. After a moment:*

SANDY
I think I figured out what's wrong with me.

CHERYL
You mean today or generally?

SANDY
What's wrong with me today?

CHERYL
"What's wrong with you today"?

SANDY
What did I do today?

CHERYL
Well you didn't speak to me but to insult me.

SANDY
How did I insult you?

CHERYL
Why would you ask me why do I even bother dying my hair? Like I'm that old what difference would it make.

SANDY
I didn't say why do you even bother.

CHERYL
Oh you did.

SANDY goes back to checking social media on her phone.

SANDY
Well why do you?

CHERYL
This is my natural hair colour.

SANDY
No, your natural hair colour is grey.

CHERYL
This is the colour I was born with.

SANDY
And now you're nearly sixty.

CHERYL
Oh my God.

SANDY
Your skin tone has changed. Your hair is too dark for your skin tone now.

CHERYL
My skin tone hasn't changed! I've been using the same foundation for thirty years!

SANDY
I think you'd look beautiful with grey hair.

CHERYL
Beautiful. Right.

SANDY
Grandma looked beautiful with grey hair.

CHERYL
Grandma was an old lady at forty for God's sake
Are you going to help me with this?

SANDY
That old actor from that detective show died.

CHERYL
I know, I saw that this morning. Your father used to like him.

SANDY
Besides that just the usual: the world on fire.

CHERYL
So what's wrong with you then, that you figured out?

SANDY
I don't know . . .

CHERYL
You don't know?

SANDY
I just . . . I need a break.

CHERYL
A break?
You're wearing pyjamas. You're wearing slippers outside the house and you need a break?

SANDY
I understand that none of this is real for you.

CHERYL
None of what?

SANDY
This whole thing, this . . . these *swings*, this *depression*, this *mania*, however they codify it . . . this thing that has really been going on longer than you know. Forever, really, as a surging and ebbing continuous kind of thing.

CHERYL
Forever?

SANDY
Since . . . God . . . fourteen?

CHERYL
You felt this way since you were fourteen?

SANDY
Maybe earlier.
And it's not like I didn't want to talk to you about it but what could you do, and then everything happened with Dad, and you

had enough on your plate, and also I know how you deal with this stuff. You go to church.

CHERYL

How I deal with it?

SANDY

And I'm not judging that, okay, it works for you so great, but as you know my way is not the way of the cross. So I dealt with it as I dealt with it—I lived with you know, I lived with it. And then there was the first psychiatrist, and that's when the diagnosis had come, which I refuted, and the first pills, which I refused. But one can only fight until one can't fight anymore. And mostly because I was working on my thesis this—this *depression*, this *mania*, this surging and ebbing was actually kind of working for me.

CHERYL

It was *working for you.*

SANDY

Yeah, for my thesis.

CHERYL

Your thesis that you took the break from?

SANDY

Exactly.
But the thesis was the real first psychiatrist in a way.

CHERYL

The thesis was a *psychiatrist*?

SANDY

In a way.

CHERYL
Did you see a lot of psychiatrists?

SANDY
No. They were mostly therapists. Just the first psychiatrist and one other. And he was creepy.

CHERYL
How was he creepy?

SANDY
He got creepy. I shouldn't have gone for beers with him.

CHERYL
You went—?

SANDY
I don't want to get into all that.
What I'm trying to tell you is—

CHERYL
You stopped taking the medication.

SANDY
What? No. What? I mean yes, but no, what I'm saying is . . .
Did Dad tell you that? Fine yes okay. But no . . .

CHERYL
It sounds like you're talking in circles to me.

SANDY
I just need a break.

CHERYL
So that's what's wrong with you?

I thought you were on a break. You need a break from your break? Does that mean you're going to get a job?

SANDY
You want me to get a job?
What kind of job would you like me to get, Mom?

CHERYL
No . . . I just . . .
If all that is real . . . and I'm not saying it's not . . . but if all that is real then why would you stop taking the pills?

SANDY
I need a break.

CHERYL
You need a drink.

SANDY
Maybe.
Maybe we all need a drink.

After a moment.

CHERYL
So you've been off the pills for a week?

SANDY
Two.

CHERYL
Well. You don't seem that different to me. Before the pills, on the pills, off the pills, when you were depressed, when you were anxious, when you were *surging*, when you were *ebbing*. You've always been moody. You're meaner maybe.

SANDY
Meaner?

CHERYL
Yeah, you're meaner than you used to be. I thought that was maybe too much university.

SANDY
Oh don't start that.

CHERYL
I think you need to go to church.

SANDY
Oh my God.

CHERYL
That's right.

SANDY
What's right?

CHERYL
Oh your God.

SANDY
Oh my God.

CHERYL
You know, your father says that you and I are a lot alike.
I don't see it.

SANDY
No I don't see that no.

DOUGIE comes out of the bedroom. He is looking spiffy in his nice shirt and his good jeans. Most noticeably he is wearing a hairpiece.

Hey, Dad.

DOUGIE
How ya doin', darling.

CHERYL
Oh, Dougie, you're not wearing that again.

DOUGIE
What? Yes I am.

SANDY
You look great, Dad.

CHERYL
What's Charky going to think of that?

DOUGIE
Charky hasn't seen me in thirty years, Cheryl. He's going to expect me to look like this.

CHERYL
He's seen pictures surely.

DOUGIE
I've always got my hat on on Facebook.

CHERYL
It's not necessary, Dougie.

SANDY
I think you look really great, Dad.

CHERYL
He looks really great?

SANDY
Yes.

CHERYL
I look like an old hag with my hair too dyed and my terrible complexion but he looks really great.

SANDY
Be nice, Mom.

DOUGIE
Yeah, be nice, Cheryl.

CHERYL
Me be nice?

SANDY AND DOUGIE
Yes.

After a moment.

CHERYL
What time does Charky get in at?

DOUGIE
Between seven and seven thirty.

CHERYL
That's when he lands or that's when he gets here?

DOUGIE
Gets here.

CHERYL
Did you get that new mattress set up?

DOUGIE
Yes.

CHERYL
Did it fit all right in that tiny room?

DOUGIE
Yes.

CHERYL heads toward the guest room.

CHERYL
Did you get it made up all right?

DOUGIE
Yes let it be, Cheryl.

CHERYL
I'm just taking a look.

CHERYL goes into the guest room.

DOUGIE
(sotto voce) She's driving me nuts!

CHERYL
(off) Oh, it looks really nice.

SANDY
(sotto voce) She'll be going to Mass soon.

CHERYL
(off) Oh this bed is so comfortable.

SANDY
That actor died, from that detective show.

DOUGIE
I saw that before.
Your mother liked him.

CHERYL
(off) What's all this?

DOUGIE
What's all what?

CHERYL
(off) All this in the closet.

DOUGIE
Why are you in the closet, Cheryl?

> CHERYL *comes out into the hallway with a box of fireworks.*

CHERYL
What's all this?

DOUGIE
Fireworks.

CHERYL
What for?

DOUGIE
For tonight. Celebrate the reunion.

CHERYL
Fireworks?

DOUGIE
We used to set off fireworks when we were kids.

CHERYL
No we didn't.

DOUGIE
Charky and me did.

CHERYL
No you didn't.

DOUGIE
Don't be telling me what we did or didn't do.

DOUGIE *takes the bag from her and exits, putting it back.*

I knew Charky long before I knew you, Cheryl. And also you don't have to be snooping. Please.

CHERYL
Is Charky's sister still living here?

DOUGIE
(returning) It's unlikely he'd be staying with me if Paula still lived here.

CHERYL
Not necessarily.

DOUGIE
Why *not necessarily*?

CHERYL
Well, I wouldn't stay with my sister if I had the chance to stay somewhere else.

DOUGIE
Yeah well Charky's not you.

SANDY
Lucky for Charky.

DOUGIE
Ha!

CHERYL
Oh yeah, me be nice.

DOUGIE
(laughing) Lucky for Charky.

CHERYL
Speaking of the Pier, apparently the mayor brought some developer in from Ontario who bought up a bunch of land down there.

DOUGIE
Oh my God, Cheryl, who cares?

CHERYL
And all this paperwork's apparently going through with nobody even seeing it.

DOUGIE
Who cares besides you and Buddy Walsh?

SANDY
Who was talking about the Pier?

CHERYL
His people aren't even originally from here that's the problem.

SANDY
Who?

DOUGIE
Where are they from?

CHERYL
(to SANDY) That rig the mayor.
(to DOUGIE) New Brunswick.

DOUGIE
That figures.

SANDY
What made you think of the Pier?

CHERYL
Charky's sister.

SANDY
What's his real name?

DOUGIE
Allen.

SANDY
Why do you call him Charky?

CHERYL
Everybody calls him Charky.

SANDY
But why?

DOUGIE
Have you not been on his Facebook? Go on his Facebook.

DOUGIE takes SANDY's phone and opens Facebook.

(to SANDY) You met him.

CHERYL
(to DOUGIE) She was five.

DOUGIE
(to CHERYL) No I know.
(to SANDY) You don't remember meeting him do ya?

SANDY
No.

DOUGIE shows SANDY the Facebook profile.

DOUGIE
There he is.

SANDY
Wait, what? Why?

DOUGIE
Why what?

SANDY
Charky?

DOUGIE
Charky. Charc. Charcoal.

SANDY
Because he's Black?

CHERYL
(to DOUGIE) Charcoal? Is that why?

DOUGIE
Yes why else?

SANDY
You can't—

CHERYL
I thought it was because you were Sparky.

SANDY
You can't—

CHERYL
Sparky and Charky.
(to SANDY) They were always together.

DOUGIE
(to CHERYL) No he was Charky before I was Sparky.

SANDY
You can't call him Charky.

CHERYL
Everybody called him Charky.

DOUGIE
His family called him Charky.

CHERYL
He's Charky in the yearbook.

SANDY
No you can't.

DOUGIE
Everybody had a nickname. They called me Sparky.

SANDY
Yeah, but they didn't call you *Pinky*.

DOUGIE
Pinky?

SANDY
Or *Whitey*.

DOUGIE
Oh, why do you gotta get like that for?

CHERYL
He called himself Charky, Sandy.

DOUGIE
(to SANDY*)* Why do you gotta turn in into that?

SANDY
Well he calls himself *Allen* on Facebook, Mom.

DOUGIE
It was long ago, it was kids, it was what you did. That kid who used to bang his head on things and he had to wear a helmet . . .

CHERYL
Jordy Gillis.

DOUGIE
Jordy Gillis. They called him Smash. 'Cause of the helmet. Bobby Crocker, he used to be really big.

CHERYL
He was.

DOUGIE
So Tubs they called him. They called me Sparky because I couldn't sit still. That's just how it was, it was what you saw. It wasn't about making anybody feel bad. He called himself Charky.

SANDY
Okay, Dad.

DOUGIE
Why is everything all about making people feel bad now? That's the Internet, that's what that is. The whole point of the Internet is to make people feel bad. The other day somebody on there putting up this terrible story about these kids over in somewhere working in this factory—terrible terrible story of bad conditions and awful treatment of these kids and everything—and people are all commenting on it like, "That's so horrible, thanks for sharing." Thanks for sharing? It's horrible, no thanks for sharing, no thanks for sharing that.

SANDY
But that's how people find out about these things.

DOUGIE
(raging, slamming the counter) Why do I need to be finding out about these things? Go tell the police, go tell the politicians. What am I supposed to do? Go over there and save them? I've got enough to do here trying to save myself.

> DOUGIE *turns away, leaning against the counter.*
>
> *Silence.*
>
> CHERYL *sarcastically gives* SANDY *a thumbs up for "good job upsetting your father."* SANDY *silently waves* CHERYL *away.*

SANDY
It's okay, Dad.

DOUGIE
I know it's okay. I know.

CHERYL
It's all right, Dougie.

DOUGIE
I know.

Silence.

DOUGIE *begins wiping the counters and sink.*

CHERYL
It's quarter to five now. I'm going to Mass.
Who's coming with me?

DOUGIE
Ha.

SANDY
Yeah, no.

CHERYL
Father Cameron is going to be there. It's his birthday coming up.
It be nice if there was a crowd.

DOUGIE
I've got all this to do here.

CHERYL
Sandy?

SANDY
No.

CHERYL
A just flat-out "no"?

SANDY
Yes. No.

CHERYL
For God's sake, Sandy, he's eighty-five years old next week.

SANDY
Next year tell him not to have his birthday party in church and I might show up for eighty-six.

DOUGIE
Ha.

CHERYL
Yeah right, me be nice.
(to SANDY) Your aunt Brenda's coming—you don't want to see your aunt?

SANDY
I saw her this morning and again after lunch.

DOUGIE
That's enough of Brenda for a month.

SANDY
Ha!

CHERYL *departs.*

CHERYL
Oh yes you're the nice ones.
I'll be back.

CHERYL is gone. After a moment.

SANDY
You all right?

DOUGIE
Yes.

SANDY
How's the pain?

DOUGIE
I'm all right.
I dropped your wine.

SANDY
I saw, no problem. I'll pick some up.

DOUGIE
Oh God, look, your mother left the macaroni and cheese out on the counter! That'll go bad!

SANDY
I got it.

SANDY puts the casserole dish in the fridge.

DOUGIE
Did she put bacon in it?

SANDY
Yeah.

DOUGIE
I don't even know if—
He's a runner now so I don't know if he eats that kind of stuff anymore.

SANDY
Do you want me to pick up some salads just in case?

DOUGIE
He doesn't care what you call him. He never cared. He never said he cared.

SANDY
Okay . . .

DOUGIE
He called himself that.

SANDY
Just ask him. What he wants to be called.

DOUGIE
I will. He'd be fine with that if I asked him. We've known each other since we were this tall. All through high school.
I'll ask him.

SANDY
Good.

SANDY is scrolling through ALLEN's social media on her phone.

DOUGIE
I'll call him Allen. I'll call him whatever he wants.
He's the best friend I ever had.

SANDY
Here he is running.

DOUGIE
Yes. I was telling your mother.

SANDY
Are these his kids?

DOUGIE
No kids, no. He was married for a while but apparently that didn't work out. He has nephews.

SANDY
What does he do?

DOUGIE
He teaches at university. Up in Toronto.

SANDY
Oh . . . really . . .

DOUGIE
You two will have lots to say.
Maybe he could get you a job.

SANDY
We'll have lots to say.

DOUGIE
Is that what you're wearing?

SANDY
No no, I'm going back to Mom's first.

DOUGIE
I mean wear what you want.

SANDY
Oh my God no. It's special. We'll all dress up.

DOUGIE
It is special.
I got a bunch to do here . . .

SANDY moves to leave.

SANDY
I'll pick up some wine. Maybe a salad.

DOUGIE
Yes good, get a salad.

SANDY
I'll see you in a while.

DOUGIE
Good.

SANDY is on her way out the door.

Love you.

SANDY
Love you too.

SANDY departs.

DOUGIE *shows the physical discomfort he has been feeling in his abdomen.*

He opens the cupboard and considers taking a pill from the oft-inspected bottle.

He decides not to.

Instead he pours himself a shot of vodka and drinks it back.

He goes to the boom box and puts on another high school hit. Perhaps Peter Frampton's "Show Me the Way."

He plays air guitar as the lights fade.

Blackout.

SCENE 2

Three hours later.

DOUGIE *fusses over the liquor bottles arranged on the kitchen table.*

He hears a car approach.

He has a quick shot and is almost caught as CHERYL *enters.*

DOUGIE
Why are you so late?

CHERYL
Oh my God. I'm having a drink. Have you had a drink yet?

DOUGIE
No.

CHERYL
Well I'm having a drink.

CHERYL *moves the bottles around on the table.* DOUGIE *dashes over to take control. He makes* CHERYL *a drink.*

DOUGIE
I'll get it, I'll get it.
Why are you so late?

CHERYL
I'm still just coming from dropping off Brenda from Mass. I didn't even get home. Oh the drama!

DOUGIE
What drama?

CHERYL
The MacNeil brother showed up. Colin MacNeil. Brenda called him Jimmy but it was Jimmy who killed himself, wasn't it?

DOUGIE
Oh my God, Cheryl, small-town soap operas, who gives a shit.

CHERYL
Yes, Colin MacNeil. Anyway. He came in late. Brenda saw him first. She leans over to me, "The gall of him coming in here," she says. I didn't know what she was talking about. Then I look back and see Colin MacNeil. He didn't say a word, didn't make a show. He just came in and sat down at the back. Father Cameron didn't do anything. He must've seen him. I didn't see him see him but he must've known he was there. At the end of Mass the church cleared out like somebody dropped a stink bomb. I told Brenda that's not right to say that—"the gall of him coming in here"—and she just spent an hour taking my head off.

DOUGIE
Yes well yes that is right, the gall of him. If all what he says said happened happened. It's not even his parish. If he's going to make all these accusations what the hell's he doing coming around for? None of those MacNeils were right in the head. That whole family.

CHERYL
That's what Brenda says.
But don't you think if he still wants to—?

DOUGIE
I don't think about it.

CHERYL
No but if he wants to keep going to Mass—

DOUGIE
Is it really important, Cheryl, to bring in all the problems of the world into this trailer today, tonight? The mayor this and the priest that and the crazy MacNeil brothers and sexism and abuse and racial issues and all the rest of it, do we really got to do all that? Can we not just leave the world out there out there tonight? 'Cause I'll tell you, I've got enough I'm dealing with right here just here on my own.

CHERYL
I know, Dougie, I'm sorry. I just—I'm sorry. Sandy shouldn't have got into all that before.

DOUGIE
It's not Sandy . . . And look I called him Charky on the phone, he didn't say anything. It doesn't matter. I'll ask him. It's fine.

CHERYL
We'll just call him Allen then.

DOUGIE
It's fine, Cheryl, Jesus, it doesn't matter.

CHERYL
Exactly.

DOUGIE
Oh my nerves.
(going to window) Where's Sandy? She said she was bringing some healthy food.

CHERYL
Healthy food? That macaroni and cheese is healthy.

DOUGIE
It's full of cheese.

CHERYL
What's wrong with cheese?

DOUGIE
Runners don't eat cheese.

CHERYL
He's not a runner.

DOUGIE
Healthy people don't eat cheese.

CHERYL
That's beautiful cheese.

DOUGIE
Or bacon.

CHERYL
Oh there's hardly bacon in there enough to notice.

DOUGIE
Bacon is bacon.

CHERYL
You're the one who wanted bacon.

We hear a car pull up.

DOUGIE
Oh oh! That might be something, that might be him. Yup yup. Might be.

CHERYL
How's he travelling?

DOUGIE
Rent-a-car from the airport. Sure it is, sure it is. It's him. Should we put on some music?

CHERYL
What music? What you got, trumpets? Have a fanfare? Should we do the fireworks now?

DOUGIE
Why are you being an arsehole, Cheryl?

CHERYL
I'm just teasing ya.

DOUGIE
Just so it wasn't too quiet that's all.

CHERYL
No worry it's going to be too quiet both of us here.

DOUGIE
There he is there he is.

ALLEN *knocks on the door.*

Come in come in come in!

CHERYL
Come on in!

ALLEN enters. He rolls a carry-on suitcase.

DOUGIE
Oh my God look at you.

ALLEN
Look at you.

DOUGIE
Come in come in.

ALLEN
Shoes on? Shoes off?

DOUGIE
Doesn't matter. Take 'em off. Doesn't matter.

ALLEN kicks off his shoes. He goes to DOUGIE. DOUGIE grips his arm hard and gives him a serious handshake.

Oh my God, look at you. Oh my God.

ALLEN
So good to see you.

DOUGIE
Oh my God. Look at you. You still got all your hair.

ALLEN
You still have . . . all your hair.

DOUGIE
Yeah yeah.

ALLEN
You have more hair than you did in high school.

DOUGIE
Yeah yeah.

CHERYL
(to ALLEN) Get over here you.

ALLEN
Cheryl.

CHERYL
Give us a hug then.

They hug.

You look so good. You feel so fit.
What are you doing? You're doing something.
Dougie, feel his arm.

DOUGIE
I know, I did.

CHERYL
You're built like a brick shithouse.

ALLEN *laughs heartily.*

Feel his arm.

DOUGIE
I did.

ALLEN
(to DOUGIE*)* You haven't gained a pound.

CHERYL
He was thinner.

DOUGIE
Cheryl . . .

ALLEN
Oh yeah?

CHERYL
But doesn't he look good?

ALLEN
He does, he does.

DOUGIE
Yeah go on.

ALLEN
You're both a sight for sore eyes.

CHERYL
Well he looks good, but me if you look too hard your eyes will get sore.

An awkward silence.

DOUGIE
Will you have a drink?

CHERYL
Let's have a—

ALLEN
Not this moment no.

DOUGIE
Okay.

ALLEN
I'd like to drop my stuff, wash my hands?

DOUGIE
Oh God yes yes, your room's just the first one there and the bathroom's the one with the light on.

ALLEN
Great.
So good to see you both.

DOUGIE
So good to see you.

ALLEN exits down the hallway. DOUGIE and CHERYL speak quietly.

CHERYL
He looks so good.

DOUGIE
I know I know.

CHERYL
His arms are like—

DOUGIE
I know.
And his skin.

CHERYL
Yes.

ALLEN *pops in briefly.*

ALLEN
Bathroom just down the hall?

DOUGIE
Yes yes.
Nothing at all to drink?

ALLEN
Right now . . . ? Sparkling water if you've got it.
Club soda?

DOUGIE
Yes yes good all right. Getting on that.

ALLEN *exits again.* DOUGIE *and* CHERYL *speak quietly.*

Text Sandy, get her to pick up some sparkling water.

CHERYL
Yes yes good good.

DOUGIE
Is he not drinking at all?

CHERYL
No just not right now I think.

DOUGIE
Just not right now not this minute or *just not right now* not tonight?

CHERYL
Not this minute.

DOUGIE
I bought too much.

CHERYL
No no.

DOUGIE
He's going to think I'm a boozer.

CHERYL
No no, it's fine, we don't have to drink it all. It's just there.

DOUGIE
(calling down hallway) We'll have that sparkling water for you shortly.
(louder) We'll have that sparkling water for you shortly.

ALLEN
(off) What's that?

DOUGIE
We're just getting that sparkling water for you.

ALLEN
(off) Very good.

DOUGIE
(to CHERYL) What's Sandy saying?

CHERYL
Nothing, I just texted her two seconds ago.
(calling down hallway) Um—uh—do—? You'll have a little drink though will you later right? Will you have a drink later on?

ALLEN *returns holding up a bottle of wine in a paper bag.*

ALLEN
Are you talking to me?

CHERYL
Oh good.

DOUGIE
Great!

ALLEN
A bottle for the house.

CHERYL
Oh good.

DOUGIE
Great great. Would you like some of this now?

ALLEN
I'll be good with water for the moment.

DOUGIE
Sandy's got the sparkling water, she's just a little late.

ALLEN
Tap water's fine.

DOUGIE
No no no no no.

CHERYL
There's little bottles in the fridge. I'll get you one.

DOUGIE
No drinking the tap water here.

ALLEN
Still?

DOUGIE
That's right, that's right, we used to get it from that spring on the Meadow Road. Fill up a couple of ten gallons there and you were good to go. Closed that up now.

ALLEN
We used to boil it.

CHERYL
(giving ALLEN *water)* There you go.

ALLEN
Thank you.
It's still a problem?

CHERYL
It got better then it got bad again, then they fixed it.

DOUGIE
They say it's fine now but I don't trust it.

ALLEN
Nothing changes.

CHERYL
Well, some things change. For better or worse.

DOUGIE
(to CHERYL*)* What do you mean by that?

CHERYL
(to DOUGIE*)* I don't mean anything.

DOUGIE
(to ALLEN*)* So what do you eat?

ALLEN
What do I eat?

DOUGIE
So you're a runner or whatever, what kind of food do you eat? Healthy food probably right?

ALLEN
Oh, I'm not a runner.

CHERYL
(to DOUGIE*)* Oh he's not.

ALLEN
I go to a boxing gym a few times a week.

DOUGIE
I saw you running on Facebook though.

ALLEN
Oh yeah, I did a half marathon.

DOUGIE
Which would be running?

ALLEN
Yeah.

DOUGIE
(to CHERYL*)* Oh okay.

ALLEN
But that was three years ago. You went that far back on Facebook?

DOUGIE
No, yeah . . . catching up.

CHERYL
Would you eat macaroni and cheese?

ALLEN
Not at the moment.

DOUGIE
(to CHERYL) No.

CHERYL
But you would eat it.

ALLEN
I would.

CHERYL
That's what I made.

DOUGIE
There's bacon in it.

ALLEN
Well who would say no to bacon once in a while.

CHERYL
That's what I say.

DOUGIE
(to CHERYL) You never say that.

ALLEN
So, Dougie, you live here.

DOUGIE
Yes.

ALLEN
And, Cheryl, you live . . . ?

CHERYL
In the house . . . The matrimonial home.

ALLEN
But you two are . . . ?

DOUGIE
Separated.

CHERYL
Technically separated.

DOUGIE
Fifteen years.

CHERYL
Hard to believe. I see more of him now than when we lived together.

ALLEN
Well if it works it works.

DOUGIE
I don't know about that.

CHERYL
It works all right.

DOUGIE
For what it is.

CHERYL
For what it is it works.

DOUGIE
I'm going to have a drink now, nobody minds.

ALLEN
No no.

CHERYL
Fill your boots.
Fact is, we didn't see that much of one another for a few years but then there was all the hospital business and the surgeries . . .

DOUGIE
God, Cheryl . . .

CHERYL
So I was coming by to help out and then we just got into a routine.

ALLEN
Maybe more people should try not living together.

CHERYL laughs elaborately.

DOUGIE
You're on your own you said yeah?

ALLEN
That I am.
This place is spotless. Unbelievable.
And it's like this all the time, isn't it, Cheryl?

CHERYL
Is it ever. Not a crumb on the counter. Not a drop of water in the sink.

ALLEN
But he wasn't always like that. When he was a kid he was a scruffy little messy little brat.

DOUGIE
No!

ALLEN
You were yes. A carefree little scamp.

DOUGIE laughs delightedly.

CHERYL
Oh he can still be a scamp.

ALLEN
Not so carefree though eh?

CHERYL
Well you know . . . we get older.

ALLEN
I've known him a long time, Cheryl. I've known him longer than you.

CHERYL
Yes you have.

ALLEN
Because I remember the carefree thing. And I remember when it changed. Twelve, thirteen. He got kind of . . . Like this.

DOUGIE
Like what?

ALLEN
Like the shoes here. I remember when this started.

DOUGIE
What?

ALLEN
All lined up perfectly like that. That's driving you crazy that my shoes are messy like that.

DOUGIE
Like what?

ALLEN
That they aren't evenly lined up.

DOUGIE
Well no . . . I never even noticed it till you said it.

ALLEN
You want to straighten them out, don't you?

DOUGIE
No. Well . . . You straighten them out. They're your shoes.

ALLEN
Doesn't bother me.

DOUGIE
Well now that you . . . Go on, straighten them out.

ALLEN
I'm good.

DOUGIE
(laughing) Goddamn it!

DOUGIE *straightens out the shoes.*

ALLEN
Am I right, Cheryl?

CHERYL
Oh don't tell me, I lived with it all my life.

DOUGIE
(laughing) Oh yes what a terrible monster I am, I want things neat and tidy.

ALLEN
(laughing) Oh, my old friend, you're no monster.

ALLEN *hugs* DOUGIE *from behind.* DOUGIE *is surprised.*

DOUGIE
Let me get to my drink now.

ALLEN *releases him.*

ALLEN
Go for it.

DOUGIE
And I'm going to ask you a question.

ALLEN
You're going to ask me a question?

DOUGIE
I am.

ALLEN
Ask away.

DOUGIE
So we were talking here earlier, talking to Sandy, talking about the old days and Charky this and Charky that. All good things, you know, about us and the past. And she's asking, you know, why'd everybody call you Charky and that, right? And so I explained to her about you know—I told her about Sparky and that.

ALLEN
Yeah but you were Sparky after—

DOUGIE
No yeah I know. So I explain to her about, you know, you and charcoal and all that. And she's, *you can't call him that.* And I'm telling her, well everybody called you that, you called yourself that. Right? Right?

ALLEN
Uh huh.

DOUGIE
So I'm just asking, you know, what do you want to be called?

ALLEN
You can call me whatever you're comfortable with, Dougie.

DOUGIE
Well what are you comfortable with?

ALLEN
What am I comfortable with?

DOUGIE
Yeah.

ALLEN
People call me Allen.

DOUGIE
Okay well good then. I mean it wasn't, you know— Everybody called you Charky. Your family called you Charky.

ALLEN
Yeah my cousins.

DOUGIE
Paula.

ALLEN
No my sister never called me Charky.

DOUGIE
Okay I didn't know that. All right. But you said it.

ALLEN
I did.

CHERYL
It was in the yearbook.

ALLEN
Yes yes, back then, a place like this, you just go with the flow. When in Rome, right? But the problem is, to survive in this kind of Rome, you actually have to become a Roman.

DOUGIE
Well isn't that good, then everybody's the same?

ALLEN
But everybody isn't.

DOUGIE
Okay . . . But . . . I like that thing where it's, you know, one race, the human race.

ALLEN
Yes sure. But it's easier for some people to see it from that perspective than others.

DOUGIE
I guess.

ALLEN
Everybody's not playing with the same rules.

DOUGIE
Okay. Okay. No yeah. I get ya. I get ya. Well there's no rules here. Come here then, come here, you.

DOUGIE envelops ALLEN in a hug.

Oh my God, you, oh my God.

DOUGIE releases the hug.

Oh my God.
Okay was that weird? That wasn't weird was it?

ALLEN
What, the hug?

DOUGIE
(laughing) No, you— No, the talk.

ALLEN
No, that was good. That's good.

CHERYL
So it's Allen then?

ALLEN
Yeah.

DOUGIE
What did you miss there, Cheryl?

CHERYL
I didn't even know it was from charcoal.

DOUGIE
We're done with all that, Cheryl.

ALLEN
I'll have that drink now.

DOUGIE
Right on.

CHERYL
You want your wine?

ALLEN
Rum and coke.

DOUGIE
Right on.

CHERYL
I'll get it.

DOUGIE
I'll get it, Cheryl.

CHERYL
(to DOUGIE*)* Then make it two.

DOUGIE
(running to get CHERYL*'s glass)* Oh my God . . .

ALLEN
You're the runner, Dougie. You still have a runner's body. You always did.

DOUGIE
Oh I don't know about that.

ALLEN
Sure, and those long feet.

DOUGIE
(laughing) My feet?

ALLEN
Yes, runner's feet. You could have been a sprinter. I always thought that.

DOUGIE
Did ya? You must have been thinking about me a lot it sounds like.

ALLEN
I still do, Dougie.

SANDY *is suddenly at the window.*

SANDY
Ding dong!

DOUGIE
Jesus!

CHERYL
Good God, where did you sneak up from?

SANDY
I took a cab.

ALLEN
(to DOUGIE*)* Do they still have just the two cabs?

CHERYL
A whole fleet, my dear. Drinking and driving's not the sport it used to be.

> SANDY *enters. She is dressed up, very put together—flattering dress, shoes with a heel. She is a little unsteady on her feet but not overly. Glowing a bit. She carries a bag with wine in it.*

Why did you take a cab?

SANDY
I had a little drink getting ready.
And I'm not taking my shoes off, they barely touched the ground, the shoes are part of the outfit.

DOUGIE
Where's the sparkling water?

> DOUGIE *delivers drinks to* SANDY *and* ALLEN.

SANDY
Hmm?

DOUGIE
Your mother texted you to pick up sparkling water.

SANDY
Oh, I didn't see that.

CHERYL
You didn't see it or you didn't want to bother?

SANDY
I didn't want to bother.
Who's drinking sparkling water?

ALLEN
(holding his drink aloft) Nobody anymore.

SANDY
Well helloooo.

DOUGIE
Allen, this is Sandy

SANDY
Allen. Yes. Hello, Allen. I've heard so much about you.

ALLEN
And you.

SANDY
A pleasure.

An awkward cheek kiss/handshake initiated by SANDY.

CHERYL
How many little drinks did you have, Sandy?

SANDY
A couple, little, I'm fine.

DOUGIE
(to CHERYL*)* Leave her be.

SANDY
Is Toronto surviving without me, Allen?

ALLEN
You know Toronto?

SANDY
We are kindred spirits, Toronto and I.
(putting her wine with the rest) Are you a wine drinker, Allen?

ALLEN
Not so much.

SANDY
Well I am, so all is good.

DOUGIE
Did you get some salads?

SANDY
Oh, that was me, wasn't it. No, sorry.

DOUGIE
So what did you bring?

SANDY
My wine. Myself. My wit.

ALLEN
Well if you get your wit from your mother and father we're in for a night.

CHERYL
I don't know where she gets this malarkey.

ALLEN
So you're home visiting?

SANDY
Yes-ish. For a while, hanging out, helping out.

ALLEN
Visiting-ish.

SANDY
Exactly.
You know, Allen, we share a language, you and I.

ALLEN
What is that?

SANDY
The language of academia.

ALLEN
Dougie mentioned you're in school.

SANDY
Yes well . . . that's not inaccurate. In and out of grad school. Working on a thesis. You're at U of T.

ALLEN
Yes I am.

SANDY
That's a good school.

ALLEN
There are good people there, yes.

SANDY
I considered them for some grad work, but Guelph offered a scholarship. You're in English.

ALLEN
I am.

SANDY
As am I. My thesis was to be on the poet Gwendolyn MacEwen and the mystic arts as related to her earlier work.

ALLEN
Okay, I've seen some stuff on that.

SANDY
Well if there's anything out there on it I've read it.

ALLEN
This was a theatre thing.

SANDY
Really? That's so interesting because I ended up forgoing my initial subject to focus on performance poetry after I did some work with Angela Rawlings. Are you familiar . . . ? A. Rawlings?

ALLEN
No . . .

SANDY
Genius stuff. Guelph hosted her at a colloqum . . . colloqeum . . . colloqUIum— Sorry, my mouth is suddenly so dry.

CHERYL
Do you want some water?

CHERYL goes to the fridge to get water for SANDY.

SANDY
I'll have a sip of wine. And water too, yes, that would be good. And so, Allen, you're in fiction.

ALLEN
Dougie, did you know all this? Did you tell Sandy—

DOUGIE
I don't even know what language ya's are talking.

SANDY
(to ALLEN) Oh you know, tic tic tic, click click click. It's all out there.

ALLEN
It is. Did you also know that I was a runner?

SANDY laughs.

CHERYL
I thought you weren't a runner.

ALLEN
I'm kidding.

SANDY
He's kidding.

DOUGIE
(to CHERYL) He's kidding.

SANDY
And you're tenured . . .

ALLEN
I am.

SANDY
. . . So you publish.

ALLEN
Mostly journals.

SANDY
And I bet there's a novel in a drawer somewhere.

ALLEN
I'm more short stories.

SANDY
Oh, okay okay. Am I getting a bit of Carveresque from you?

ALLEN
Not so much. More . . . Edward P. Jones.

SANDY
Um . . .

ALLEN
American?

SANDY
It's vaguely . . .

ALLEN
Lost In The City?

SANDY
I shall investigate.

DOUGIE
Sandy used to write beautiful poetry. She wrote one for me once. It was in a book. She had it like "to my father" on it and everything. It was unbelievable it was so beautiful. *(verklempt)* It was like she could see into my heart.

CHERYL
Dougie . . .

DOUGIE
All these years . . . and Sandy here and, Allen, you here, and the two of you getting along like a house on fire. It's really something isn't it, Cheryl?

CHERYL
It's something.

DOUGIE
Do that poem for Allen, Sandy.

SANDY
No, Dad.

DOUGIE
You know it, you did it off by heart a bunch of times.

SANDY
No, Dad.

DOUGIE
Off by heart up on stage up at St. FX.

SANDY
(to ALLEN*)* Blue Heron Writers Festival.

DOUGIE *leaps up to fetch his laptop.*

DOUGIE
There's a video of it on YouTube.

SANDY
No. Dad?

DOUGIE
I know part of it.

SANDY
Dad . . .

DOUGIE
"I Carry You With Me." That's what it's called.

DOUGIE *opens the laptop.*

ALLEN
(to SANDY*)* After *cummings*?

SANDY
(to ALLEN*)* After *cummings*. An homage.

CHERYL
(to SANDY*)* A what?

DOUGIE
"Once there was a village . . .
Once some people made a village . . .
Now burnt to an ember."

SANDY
Dad . . .

DOUGIE
"Warm like your heart."

ALLEN
I sense the *cummings*.

SANDY
It's more his sentiment than his style.

DOUGIE
Then something about not being afraid of time because sadness is joy and going home. I don't remember it exactly. And then "I carry you with me."

> SANDY *takes the laptop from* DOUGIE *and closes it, leaving it on the coffee table.*

SANDY
Okay, Dad.

DOUGIE
That's how it ends.

SANDY
Something like that.

DOUGIE
(verklepmt) It always gets me right in the heart.

CHERYL
Dougie . . .

ALLEN
Always been a softie hasn't he, Cheryl.

CHERYL
He can go there he can.

ALLEN
And that's a good thing.

SANDY
Yes it is a good thing.

ALLEN
Sandy, would you like to see your father when he was a kid?

SANDY
Would I?!

DOUGIE
What? When? Show me.

ALLEN
Hang on a second.

ALLEN goes to his room.

DOUGIE
(delighted) Oh my God, what's this going to be?

CHERYL
Get a grip on yourself, Sandy.

SANDY
What?

DOUGIE
What?

CHERYL
Stop monopolizing him.

DOUGIE
She's not monopolizing him.

SANDY
I'm not.

DOUGIE
Leave her be. They're talking about people and stuff that they know. He's a grown man, if he doesn't want to talk to her he won't.

CHERYL
All right. Why do I bother?

DOUGIE
I don't know why sometimes, honest to God, Cheryl, I don't.

ALLEN returns. He is holding a DVD.

ALLEN
Can you play this?

DOUGIE
What is it?

ALLEN
You'll see. Can you play it?

DOUGIE
On my computer.

ALLEN
Great.

> DOUGIE *grabs his laptop from the coffee table.*

CHERYL
What is it?

DOUGIE
Oh shit, I can't play it. The side thing's broken.

SANDY
(to DOUGIE*)* That's what the external drive is for.

DOUGIE
The what?

SANDY
The thing I bought you for Christmas.

DOUGIE
Oh right.

> DOUGIE *retrieves a* CD *drive from a cupboard in the kitchen, still in the package.*

What is it, Allen?

CHERYL
What is it, Allen?

ALLEN
New Magic Valley Fun Town.

SANDY
What's that?

CHERYL
Oh my God, I haven't thought about that place in years.

SANDY
What is it?

DOUGIE
(to ALLEN) Where'd you get that?

CHERYL
(to SANDY) Just a place for the kids.
(to ALLEN) It would've closed long before she was born.

ALLEN
(to CHERYL) Oh for sure.

DOUGIE
(to ALLEN) Where'd you get that?

ALLEN
(to DOUGIE) I had it.

DOUGIE
(to ALLEN) You always had it?

ALLEN
Yeah.
Play it.

DOUGIE
Play it now?

ALLEN
Yes.
There's nothing to be scared of.

SANDY
(re: external drive) Give me, I'll do it.
New Magic what?

SANDY takes the drive from DOUGIE and the DVD from ALLEN. Over the course of the scene she takes the drive from its box and connects it to the laptop.

CHERYL
New Magic Valley Fun Town.

DOUGIE
(to ALLEN) What's *on* it?

ALLEN
(to DOUGIE) Just us being kids.

SANDY
Where was it?

CHERYL
(to SANDY) Out past the Meadow Road.

DOUGIE
(to ALLEN) What's on it?

ALLEN
(to DOUGIE) It's just us being foolish. It's from the first time we went out there.

DOUGIE
(to ALLEN) Oh, okay.

SANDY
Like an amusement park?

CHERYL
Yes. For fun. For kids. A haunted house. A swimming pool with a big slide—but then they couldn't use the slide because the pool wasn't deep enough and people kept banging their arse on the bottom.

SANDY
Where was the valley?

CHERYL
There was no valley, that was just because the old quarry was out near there.

SANDY
A quarry's not a valley.

CHERYL
Well I guess "Magic Valley" sounded better than "Magic Quarry."

ALLEN
It wasn't "Magic" originally.

CHERYL
Oh that's right, it was "Ghost," wasn't it? Because of the haunted house. New Ghost Valley Fun Town

ALLEN
That's right.

CHERYL
New Ghost Valley Fun Town. But a couple of the churches didn't like "Ghost" because of Satanism being the big thing back then,

so they changed it to "Magic." Some of the churches didn't like "Magic" even. The Catholics didn't care about "Magic" though.

SANDY
Catholics love magic.

CHERYL
(to SANDY) Watch yourself.

SANDY
Why "Town"?

DOUGIE
Oh they were going to put in some kind of mini main street for the little ones but that never happened.

SANDY
Why "New"?

DOUGIE
It was always "New."

SANDY
In relation to what?

DOUGIE
In relation to not having been there at all I guess.

CHERYL
It was just always "New." It was "New" till it got old. It was "New" till it closed. It's still "New" now. New Magic Valley Fun Town.

SANDY has inserted the DVD into the drive.

She plays it.

ALLEN
(looking at the laptop) There we are.

We hear tinny sounds of excited children.

ALLEN beckons DOUGIE over.

Everyone gathers.

CHERYL
Look at you two.
Oh my God.

SANDY
Oh my God.

CHERYL
Oh my heart.

SANDY
(to ALLEN) How old are you there?

DOUGIE
Twelve.

CHERYL
Look at you! Right up in the camera!

ALLEN
Dougie loved that camera.

We hear a young boy's voice: "Make a muscle."

CHERYL
"Make a muscle"!
Look at you making a muscle.

You're like a beanpole.
Look at you run.

ALLEN
(to DOUGIE*)* Who's the runner?

DOUGIE
(to ALLEN*)* You always had this?

CHERYL
Shh!

ALLEN
(quietly) Yeah.

CHERYL
What are you doing now?

SANDY
Shh!

We hear two young voices singing a raucous hit of the day. Perhaps Elton John's "Crocodile Rock."

CHERYL
Look at you.

DOUGIE
Okay that's enough.

DOUGIE *closes the laptop.*

CHERYL AND SANDY
Nooooo.

DOUGIE
That's enough.
Thank you for the stroll down memory lane.

ALLEN
Keep it, that's for you.

SANDY
(to CHERYL*)* We'll watch the rest of it later.

DOUGIE
We'll see.
Let's have a drink.

SANDY
Let's have a dance!

SANDY *and* CHERYL *run to the boom box.*

CHERYL
My pick!

SANDY
My pick!

SANDY *shows* CHERYL *her choice.*

CHERYL
Yes!

Blackout.

We hear the original version of the song the boys were singing.

SCENE 3

An hour later.

Everyone is dancing. A new song. Perhaps "Thank You" by Sly and the Family Stone.

CHERYL*'s moves are those of a woman who has known a dance floor well but not recently.* DOUGIE *has a tight but decent rhythm.* ALLEN *is a bit stiff, the moves of a man who has spent too much time at the gym.* SANDY *is fluid and loose.*

SANDY *dances with* DOUGIE. CHERYL *dances with* ALLEN.

Everybody's doing their best, lost in the music for a few moments.

Soon SANDY *manoeuvres to dance with* ALLEN *but* CHERYL *won't give way.*

DOUGIE *takes a break to have a drink.*

There is a mild battle for position between CHERYL *and* SANDY *but neither will relent.*

Eventually ALLEN *finds his out and slips between* CHERYL *and* SANDY*, joining* DOUGIE *for a drink.*

CHERYL and SANDY dance together with some reluctance.

ALLEN and DOUGIE speak over the music.

ALLEN
It's cozy. The trailer is cozy.

DOUGIE
Cozy? What's that code for in Toronto, *small*?

ALLEN
No. It's not that small.
By Toronto standards it's palatial.

CHERYL turns the song off.

CHERYL
New song!

SANDY
New song new partner!

SANDY rushes to ALLEN.

DOUGIE
You like Toronto?

ALLEN
Toronto has its charms.

DOUGIE
Has its charms. What's that code for?

ALLEN
It's become home.

CHERYL *puts on a disco hit. Perhaps Peaches & Herb's "Shake Your Groove Thing."*

SANDY *pulls* ALLEN *out onto the dance floor.*

DOUGIE
No, here's home.

ALLEN *makes an attempt to shake his groove thing but* SANDY *seems to be dancing more for him than with him and this throws him a bit.*

As the song continues CHERYL *gets more and more into it.* DOUGIE *is dancing in the kitchen.* CHERYL *catches his eye and calls him to the floor. At first he resists but then agrees. He calls the others to clear the floor.*

Watch and be amazed.

As the music hits its stride DOUGIE *and* CHERYL *go into their routine. This is a kind of dancing they have done much in the past. Old-fashioned disco dancing. One gets the sense this is where they were at their best together physically. This is where they found sensuality with one another.*

ALLEN *and* SANDY *cheer them on. The song ends and* ALLEN *and* SANDY *hoot and holler for* DOUGIE *and* CHERYL.

Exhausted, CHERYL *hangs off* DOUGIE*'s shoulders. She looks up facing him.*

CHERYL
I might have to take you home with me.

DOUGIE
(embarrassed) Cheryl.
Cheryl.
Settle down.

CHERYL *steps back from* DOUGIE.

CHERYL
Oh my. Shame on me, behaving like we're married.

Silence.

DOUGIE *is further embarrassed.*

DOUGIE
I need a breath.

DOUGIE *departs.*

SANDY
(to CHERYL*)* Can't we just have a nice night?

CHERYL
My wish as well.

SANDY *moves to exit after her father.*

Oh go on after him.

SANDY
That's not fair, Mom.

SANDY *departs.*

CHERYL
We always gotta be so careful of Dougie.

ALLEN
Why is that, Cheryl?

CHERYL
God knows if I don't, Allen.

ALLEN
We've all got our damage.

CHERYL
He can get so cold. She's got that too. Not as bad. He can shut you right out, leave you in the dark, make you disappear so hard you have to go find a mirror just to make sure you're still there. Sandy calls it depression.
So I'd reach out to him, to be loving or kind or whatever, and the more I tried the more he'd resent it. I'd try to show him some warmth, and I might as well be sticking him with a knife. Wincing. Wincing at me.

ALLEN
Was he always like that?

CHERYL
I don't know . . . It's better now. Apart like this . . . it's better. It feels like at least now we like one another again.

ALLEN
Ah *love*, such a beautiful thing.

CHERYL
Ah love.

From outside we hear DOUGIE *and* SANDY *laugh.*

He thinks Sandy and me are alike, but God, they're two peas.

ALLEN
I see you in her too.

After a moment:

CHERYL
You look good.

ALLEN
It's a lot of work. Everything hurts.

CHERYL
Are you happy?

ALLEN
Off and on.

CHERYL
Never had kids?

ALLEN
No.

CHERYL
Never wanted them?

ALLEN
I wouldn't say that.

DOUGIE *and* SANDY *enter laughing.*

SANDY
Has the dust settled?

DOUGIE
Be careful, Allen, my ex-wife's a woman on the make tonight.

CHERYL
Arsehole.

SANDY
Okay, Dad, you're the DJ again.

> DOUGIE *is making himself a drink.*

DOUGIE
Oh no, darling, let's give the dancing a break.

> SANDY *tries to pull* ALLEN *up to dance but he is dead weight.*

ALLEN
Oh I don't think so, Sandy, I'm feeling a bit of an old man now.

CHERYL
Apparently so would she like to be.

SANDY
Mother!

DOUGIE
Don't be gross, Cheryl.

SANDY
We're just trying to have a bit of fun.

> SANDY *continues to tug on* ALLEN *but he isn't moving.*

> SANDY *loses her grip and falls back on her butt.*

ALLEN
Whoa whoa whoa.

DOUGIE
You all right?

CHERYL
Watch yourself, Sandy.

SANDY
(laughing) I'm fine I'm fine.

DOUGIE
(laughing) That's what you get for leaving your shoes on.

SANDY
I'm fine.

CHERYL
You're cut off, my dear.

SANDY
I'm fine. I'm not drunk. I haven't had a drink in an hour and all this dancing has sweated it out.

CHERYL
We should go.

SANDY
Noooo.

CHERYL
It's after midnight, Sandy.

SANDY
Noooo.

CHERYL
Well I'm going to go. I don't know how you're getting home.

SANDY
I'll take a cab.

CHERYL
She's made of money tonight.

SANDY
I'm going to have some of your macaroni and cheese.

SANDY becomes intensely focused on the macaroni and cheese.

CHERYL
Finally someone.

DOUGIE
Hey, I had some before. I told you it was delicious.

ALLEN
Yes, delicious.

CHERYL
Thank you, Allen.

DOUGIE
Oh I see . . . Don't be like that.

CHERYL
Me be like that?

ALLEN
Now now, you two, get along.

CHERYL
I'm getting along, out the door and home.

DOUGIE
Hang on hang on. Don't be mad.

CHERYL
I'm not mad. I don't care.

DOUGIE
Leave her have a bite and see how she feels then about going. We can step outside for a minute. Step outside for one.

CHERYL
I could step outside for one.

ALLEN
People are stepping outside?

DOUGIE
Cheryl has a cigarette once in awhile.

CHERYL
I have a cigarette?

DOUGIE
You do.

CHERYL
Once in a while.

ALLEN
That's all right. In moderation.

CHERYL
He's the one who's smoking who shouldn't be smoking.

> *Behind* SANDY'S *back* DOUGIE *gives* CHERYL *the sign to stop talking.* SANDY *catches this.*

SANDY
Do what you want.

DOUGIE
(to SANDY*)* In moderation.
It's not like I'm going to do any more harm than's been done.

CHERYL
You just had one outside.

DOUGIE
No I didn't. Sandy won't let me smoke.

SANDY
Do what you want.

CHERYL
If Dr. Azim knew you were smoking —

DOUGIE
You tell on me I'm telling on you.

CHERYL
What do I do with him, Allen?

ALLEN
Enjoy life.

DOUGIE
Okay, let's go outside, enjoy life in moderation for a minute before I rip my fucking eyeballs out.

CHERYL
Ten minutes and I'm gone, Sandy.

DOUGIE and CHERYL exit.

After a few moments.

SANDY
(re: macaroni and cheese) This. Is. So. Good.

ALLEN
You should tell her that.

SANDY
I know I know. Mothers and daughters. We're all destined to play out our roles.

ALLEN
You're a fatalist?

SANDY stops eating and takes a position sitting on the counter, close to ALLEN. ALLEN keeps his position.

SANDY
Oh my God. I'm going to cry. Thank you. My brain is so hungry for anything that isn't gossip or small talk. I am so starved for conversation with someone who isn't from here.

ALLEN
I'm from here.

SANDY
And yet not. You know the terrain from afar. Which makes you pretty much perfect.

ALLEN
Perfect? For . . . ?

SANDY
Pretty much anything.

ALLEN
Do you have you own . . . *(place here).*

SANDY
Do I have my own . . . ?

ALLEN
Ah . . .

SANDY
Uh huh?

ALLEN
Here's what I'm like: I want to get to know any woman I meet. It doesn't matter whose wife she is, whose daughter she is. And then once I get to know her, I forget her like she never was.

SANDY
At least you know what you're like.
Maybe I'm like that too.
Nothing has to get heavy.

ALLEN
I don't do this anymore.

SANDY
Don't do what?

ALLEN
Act out.

SANDY
Is that what we're doing?

ALLEN
It's not my business to identify what you're doing.

SANDY
You have my permission, analyze my actions.

ALLEN
Okay.

SANDY
What am I acting out over?

ALLEN
Your father.

SANDY
Oh are you getting Freudian? That's so disappointing.

ALLEN
Not so Freudian, more *12 Steps*.

SANDY
Oh. *Recovery.*

ALLEN
Recovery.

SANDY
(indicating ALLEN*'s drink)* You're on hiatus from recovery?

ALLEN
Drinking wasn't my problem.

SANDY
Aha.

> ALLEN *moves away from* SANDY.

ALLEN
And so I step away.

SANDY
Aha.

ALLEN
Okay?

SANDY
Yes. Of course. It's all good, Allen, it's all good. No drama. Just an open-minded free-spirited gal here. Polyamorous, polysexual, polly wants a cracker. No drama, all good. "We're here for a good time not a long time." Trooper, my introduction to modern Canadian poetry. Or as Queen Gwendolyn said: "With legs and arms I make alphabets." So let's say . . . I'm a communicator. That's what I'm like.

ALLEN
If that makes you happy.

SANDY
Happy? Is that the quest?

ALLEN
If it brings you peace.

SANDY
What brings you peace, Allen?

ALLEN
That's what I'm here for.

SANDY
Revisiting something.

ALLEN
Yeah.

SANDY
A lost childhood.

ALLEN
Maybe.

SANDY
All is good, Allen, all is good.

> SANDY *sits on the sofa and opens the laptop. We hear the boys singing a moment. She turns the sound down so her father won't hear it outside.*

This is adorable.
Why didn't he want us to see it? What does he do that's so embarrassing?

ALLEN
Nothing on this one. This was just the first one.

SANDY
The first one?

ALLEN
The first of many. I had them all transferred.

SANDY
Look at him playing to the camera.

ALLEN
He loved that camera.

SANDY
Do you still have it?

ALLEN
The camera belonged to the person who shot it.

SANDY
Who shot it?

ALLEN
Gordon Cameron.

SANDY
Father Cameron?

ALLEN
Yeah.

SANDY
Oh.

ALLEN
Cameron always had the newest toys.

SANDY
Oh.

SANDY closes the laptop.

Did you go to St. Margaret's too?

ALLEN
No. We were Baptist. But my father did the gardening and the grounds at St. Margaret's and the rectory. I worked summers with my father from the time I was ten. That's how I met Dougie. He was an altar boy. He spent a lot of time around the church.

And the rectory. Your father was favoured by Cameron. And then so was I.

SANDY
Favoured?

ALLEN
Trips to Fun Town. To the beach. Then parties at the rectory. Cameron liked to party. We'd go to the store to buy his mix, he'd let us hang around and drink.

SANDY
A priest would let you drink?

ALLEN
It was encouraged.

SANDY
Encouraged?

ALLEN
Oh yes.

SANDY
Father Cameron?

ALLEN
Yes.

SANDY
You and my father?

ALLEN
Yes.

Silence.

SANDY
Do you know about the brothers?

ALLEN
Jimmy and Colin MacNeil.

SANDY
You know about that?

ALLEN
I do.

SANDY
Do you know it to be true?

ALLEN
I do.

SANDY
Does my father know it to be true?

ALLEN
He does.

SANDY
Is that why you're here?

ALLEN
Yes.

SANDY
Does my father know that's why you're here?

DOUGIE
(off) Why doesn't it feel like this *before* I smoke one?!

DOUGIE comes in followed by CHERYL.

ALLEN
Not yet.

DOUGIE
It's so gross. Now. *After* I smoked one. Why can't I remember it's going to feel like this after I smoke before I smoke?

CHERYL
Oh my God, Dougie, if you're gonna bother smoking you can't beat yourself up over it every time.

DOUGIE
Augh, and the smell.

SANDY
I have to go.

CHERYL
You hafta go?

DOUGIE
That was fast.

SANDY
I just— No— I just—don't feel . . .

DOUGIE
You don't feel good?

SANDY
Yeah—my stomach.

DOUGIE
I knew it, Cheryl, you left that macaroni and cheese out on the counter.

CHERYL
What?

DOUGIE
I'm all right so far. You had some too. Are you all right, Allen?

ALLEN
Oh yeah yeah.

CHERYL
There's nothing wrong with that macaroni and cheese.

SANDY
It's not the food. I just drank too much.

CHERYL
She just drank too much.

SANDY
We've got to go.

CHERYL
Oh my God, listen to bossy.

SANDY
I just—I can't—I have to go.

DOUGIE
Are you all right?

SANDY
Yes yes.
Allen, it was such a pleasure to meet you. And thank you.
And . . .

ALLEN
And I'll see you tomorrow.

SANDY
And I'll see you tomorrow. I will see you tomorrow.
Let's go, Mom.

CHERYL
Good God, girl, let me get my shoes on.

DOUGIE
Goodnight then.

SANDY
Yes, goodnight.
I'll see you tomorrow—I'll see you tomorrow too.

CHERYL
(to ALLEN*)* Give me a hug.

They hug.

SANDY
(leaving) Come on, Mom.

CHERYL
Oh my God.
I'll see you in the morning.

ALLEN
Probably more like afternoon.

CHERYL
Yes, probably more like afternoon.

CHERYL departs after SANDY.

We hear the car start up and depart.

DOUGIE
Now here we are two, just me and you.
Another drink?

ALLEN
A splash.

DOUGIE
Got tons of music too. Got all the old CDs out.
(looks out the window) Long gone they are.
(locks the door) Nobody's going anywhere tonight anymore are they.

ALLEN
No plans to, no.

DOUGIE
No, me neither.
(re: his shirt) God that smoke stinks! I hate it.
I'm just gonna—

DOUGIE opens his shirt—he is wearing an undershirt.

I hate how it clings to ya.
Disgusting. Bad stuff, bad stuff.
You want some music?

ALLEN
Whatever you want.

DOUGIE
I've got a ton of it so why not.
(handing drink to ALLEN*)* Incoming.

ALLEN
Thanks.

> DOUGIE *puts some soft rock on the boom box. Possibly America's "Tin Man."*

> ALLEN *plays air guitar.*

> DOUGIE *grooves a bit. He sits beside* ALLEN.

> DOUGIE *is awkwardly silent but happy.*

DOUGIE
I bought fireworks.

ALLEN
Fireworks?

DOUGIE
Remember we had a plan to steal some fireworks . . .

ALLEN
That was your plan.

DOUGIE
Yeah but we had the plan to set them off.

ALLEN
There was a lot of talk about fireworks.

DOUGIE
Yeah.
These are good ones. Top dollar.

ALLEN
Maybe tomorrow.

DOUGIE
Yeah.
It's so good to see you.

ALLEN
You too.

DOUGIE
I think about you all the time.

ALLEN
You too.

DOUGIE slaps ALLEN's leg. They laugh.

He slaps ALLEN's leg again. He leaves his hand there.

ALLEN pats DOUGIE's hand. DOUGIE takes that as a sign.

DOUGIE leans in to kiss ALLEN.

ALLEN moves away.

Doug, no, Doug.

DOUGIE recoils and leaps up.

DOUGIE
Oh God oh God oh God, no no no no no no no no.

ALLEN
It's all right, Dougie, it's all right.

DOUGIE
That didn't happen. I didn't do that. That didn't happen.

> DOUGIE *is pacing back and forth, hitting himself on the head.*

ALLEN
It's all right, Dougie.

DOUGIE
No no no no no no no no.

ALLEN
Dougie, come on now.

> DOUGIE *strides off to the bedroom. He returns with the box of fireworks, striding toward the front door.*

Dougie . . .
It's all right. Dougie?
Where are you going?

> DOUGIE *steps onto the front porch and tosses the fireworks onto the lawn.*

What's that? Dougie?
You don't have to throw them away.

> DOUGIE *returns to pacing and hitting himself on the head again.*

DOUGIE
Fucker fucker fucker.

ALLEN grabs DOUGIE by the wrists to stop him.

ALLEN
Dougie, stop it. Dougie, look at me, look at me.
We're soldiers right, Dougie. Remember? We're soldiers. Right?
Right?

DOUGIE
Yes, yes, right, I know, I know.

ALLEN
You got any soldier music for us, Dougie? Put some soldier music on. Come on. You must have some soldier music there.

DOUGIE
Yeah I do, I do. Here.

DOUGIE finds a song on a CD and puts it on the boom box.

ALLEN
Something good. Good for soldiers.

DOUGIE
Yeah, here, good.

An upbeat, mosh-type song comes on. Possibly the Clash's "Train in Vain."

ALLEN
That's the one. That's a good one. That's a good soldier song.
Come on, Dougie. Come on.

ALLEN and DOUGIE dance pogo style. They wildly thrash around the living room yelling as the song builds in volume.

Blackout.

SCENE 4

The mosh song is replaced by something classical in a minor chord. Perhaps Bach's Cello Suite No. 2 in D Minor.

The next afternoon.

ALLEN *sits working on his laptop with his earbuds in.*

His suitcase sits, packed, nearby.

After a moment DOUGIE *comes out of his bedroom. He is looking worse for wear just having risen, a bathrobe over pyjama bottoms and a* T*-shirt, no hairpiece.*

ALLEN *sees* DOUGIE *and pulls out his earbuds. The music stops.*

ALLEN
Hello there.

DOUGIE
Is it really two o'clock?

ALLEN
Almost.

DOUGIE
Jesus . . .

ALLEN
Cheryl came by earlier but I told her you were fine and we're just going to hang out today.

DOUGIE
I don't know how fine I am.

ALLEN
You all right?

DOUGIE
Oh my head.

ALLEN
Me too.
Have some water.

ALLEN gets a bottle of water from the fridge.

DOUGIE
(re: suitcase) You leaving?

ALLEN
I talked to my sister this morning.

DOUGIE
Where's Paula?

ALLEN
Still here.

DOUGIE
I never see her around.

ALLEN
You get to the Pier much?

DOUGIE
Not so much.

ALLEN
And she doesn't come over town much so . . .
I'll still be around, just going to stay with her for a few days.

DOUGIE
Because of last night?

ALLEN
No. Because of me and my sister.

DOUGIE
I don't hardly remember what happened—

ALLEN
It's okay, Dougie.

After a moment.

DOUGIE
That wasn't really my hair.

ALLEN
I see that. You look better like this.

DOUGIE
Right.
Oh my head.
(sitting) Oh my everything.

ALLEN
That's probably more the age than the booze.

DOUGIE
No that's probably the cancer.

ALLEN
Can we talk about that?

DOUGIE
Sure yeah. First it was a melanoma but they got that, and then it was on my bladder so they scraped that three times and did two more biopsies and two rounds of chemo. Then it was on one of my kidneys so they took that out. Now it's back on the bladder.

ALLEN
So . . . ?

DOUGIE
Maybe surgery but they say I'm not a good candidate because of the kidney.

ALLEN
So . . . ?

DOUGIE
The end.

ALLEN
And what does that look like?

DOUGIE
You mean in the end? How does it end?

ALLEN
Yeah.

DOUGIE
Well.
Nobody around here wants to talk about that. Everybody around here wants to talk about what kind of treatments, external beam radiotherapy or non-invasive some other bullshit, and who's your surgeon and which anaesthesiologist. Jesus. Everybody sounds like they got a diploma, or play some part on a medical show. You can't even get the doctors to talk about how does it end.

ALLEN
Do you want to talk about that?

DOUGIE
If the bladder doesn't come out? Two years I managed to get one of 'em to say.
I'm not having another surgery.

ALLEN
And how do you feel about that?

DOUGIE
Fucking amazing.
Remember we used to say that? When everything was shit? How was class, how was the exam, how was the party?

DOUGIE AND ALLEN
Fucking amazing.

ALLEN
It's good to talk about stuff.
Do you talk to Cheryl about it?

DOUGIE
Cheryl, oh she'd be the star of the medical show.

ALLEN
I bet Sandy would talk about it.

DOUGIE
Probably. But she's my daughter so . . .

ALLEN
Why did you buy fIreworks?

DOUGIE
Oh Jesus, I didn't set them off did I?

ALLEN
No. You threw them out on the lawn.

DOUGIE
Right.

ALLEN
Some kids came and took them this morning.

DOUGIE
Fucking kids.

ALLEN
No, they came to the door. They asked permission. I said it was okay.

DOUGIE
They'll be over in MacKenzie's field with those tonight I bet. Cops won't like that.

ALLEN
Why did you buy fireworks?

DOUGIE
Why?

ALLEN
Cameron started the fireworks talk. That's how he'd got us to the beach the first time. That's how he got us out to Crow's Creek camping for the weekend. Fucker never set off a fucking firecracker.

DOUGIE
No.

ALLEN
Were you thinking of Cameron when you bought them?

DOUGIE
No, b'y. I don't think about him.

ALLEN
How can you not?

DOUGIE
Easy.

ALLEN
You never talked to anyone?

DOUGIE
No. Who?

ALLEN
I told my sister.

DOUGIE
When?

ALLEN
Three . . . four years ago. It was a drink and dial.

DOUGIE
You told her everything?

ALLEN
I told her enough.

DOUGIE
What did Paula say?

ALLEN
She insisted I go to the authorities. But I wasn't ready. She didn't get it. We didn't talk after that. Then she emailed me a couple of months ago to tell me about Jimmy MacNeil's suicide.

DOUGIE
Everybody doesn't believe it was suicide.

ALLEN
What do you believe?

Silence.

DOUGIE
Where'd you get that video?

ALLEN
I took it. From Cameron's. I took them all.

DOUGIE
All of 'em?
When did you take 'em?

ALLEN
After we stopped going I went back. He'd call or come after me and I'd go. And every time I went I'd take one of them. I was so afraid of getting caught I would only take one at a time. And then when I had them all I stopped going.

DOUGIE
You went back on your own?

ALLEN
I did.

DOUGIE
How many was there?

ALLEN
Fifteen.

DOUGIE
Jesus.

ALLEN
I didn't know what else to do.

DOUGIE
Jesus.
He never knew you took 'em?

ALLEN
If he did I never heard.

DOUGIE
Did you watch 'em?

ALLEN
Not all of them.
My lawyer did.
She says I should take them to the police here.

After a moment.

DOUGIE
I know why you're here. I knew why you were coming.
Time. Time. And time . . . Fucking time.
All this stuff changes, *(slapping his body)* all this stuff changes, but this stuff, *(slapping his head)* but this stuff, nothing changes, nothing changes, nothing changes.

ALLEN
Dougie . . .

DOUGIE
(angry) What?
(slapping his head again) Nothing changes.

ALLEN
Dougie—

DOUGIE
Jesus, Allen . . . Why?

ALLEN
Dougie—

DOUGIE
Why?

ALLEN
Dougie—

DOUGIE
Why? What's the fucking point now? He's almost ninety years old.

ALLEN
So what about the MacNeils?

DOUGIE
That whole family was never right in the head.

ALLEN
So Colin MacNeil is just an angry gay alcoholic who wants to make a good priest look bad?
So Jimmy MacNeil is just some drug addict who OD'd?

DOUGIE
He was a drug addict.

ALLEN
Because of what happened with Cameron. It's why he took drugs. It's why I cut my family off. It's why I drove away every good woman who would have me. It's why you live out here in the middle of nowhere in a trailer.

DOUGIE
There's nothing wrong with where I live. I like it.

ALLEN
Why? Why do you like it?

DOUGIE
I like it.

ALLEN
So you can be alone.

DOUGIE
I like to be alone!

ALLEN
Cameron did that to us.
It's why we push everyone away.

DOUGIE
Look. I don't want any part of this.
I don't want to go through all that, all right?

ALLEN
So who's coming forward?
It'll just be the dead drug addict, and his drunk brother, and the Black guy?

DOUGIE
You're not *the Black guy.*

ALLEN
Who am I?

DOUGIE
You're—

ALLEN
Charky?

DOUGIE
No, you're Allen. You're Allen.

ALLEN
Not here I'm not. Not in this town.
The fear here. You can smell it. Every town like this.
And it's fear like this that runs the world now.
Somebody has to stand up. Somebody has to tell the truth.

DOUGIE
You can say whatever you want about me when I'm dead. What's two years.

ALLEN
How do you want those two years to be, Dougie?
What do you want your life to look like?
Sitting here turning to dust in your double-wide tomb?
You need to tell the truth.

DOUGIE
And then what?

ALLEN
Go back to your house, go back to Cheryl.

DOUGIE
I don't want to be with Cheryl like that.

ALLEN
Then go online and meet some guy.

DOUGIE
Oh Jesus . . .

ALLEN
Or get a goddamn dog.
Just let something love you.

Silence.

I'm going to Paula's. I'll be around. I'll wait to hear from you.

ALLEN goes to his suitcase and takes out a small stack of DVDs. He places them on the coffee table. He prepares to leave.

New Magic Valley Fun Town.
Every single one is labelled that. All the first bunch he shot out there, but then even the ones from the beach, from the parties at the rectory, camping. I guess it's how he hid it. From himself even, maybe? But it's so perfect. The lie of it. That place. It wasn't new, wasn't magic, wasn't a valley, there was no town and it wasn't fucking fun.

> DOUGIE *kisses* ALLEN. ALLEN *doesn't reciprocate but he also doesn't stop* DOUGIE. DOUGIE *moves away.*

DOUGIE
I loved you.

ALLEN
Maybe.

> ALLEN *puts on his shoes and gets his suitcase.*

DOUGIE
I still love you.

ALLEN
Maybe.
Or maybe we're just soldiers who fought in a war together.

DOUGIE
I love you.

ALLEN
Then do this for me.

> ALLEN *leaves.*

> DOUGIE *paces the trailer like an animal in a cage. He straightens up the counter but stops that. He goes to the*

pill cupboard but stops himself. He goes to have a shot but stops that. He goes to the boom box to play music but stops that. He stops and looks at the pile of DVDs *that* ALLEN *left.*

After a moment DOUGIE *picks up one and opens it.*

We hear the voices of the two boys laughing and splashing in a pool.

Children playing.

SCENE 5

Early evening.

The trailer is dim. DOUGIE's *laptop glows.* DOUGIE *stands in the kitchen, still in his pyjama bottoms but now in a hoodie. He clutches a battered chapbook in his hands.*

CHERYL *and* SANDY *enter.*

CHERYL
I don't even know if they're here.
Dougie?
What are you doing standing in the dark?
Turn some lights on, Sandy.

SANDY *does so.*

SANDY
Where's Allen, Dad?

CHERYL
Where's Allen, Dougie?

DOUGIE
He's gone to Paula's.

CHERYL
(to SANDY*)* I told you she still lived here.
(to DOUGIE*)* Is it bad or good he's gone to see her?

DOUGIE
It's good.

SANDY
You all right, Dad?

CHERYL
What are you just standing there for?

DOUGIE
We got to face what's going on, Cheryl.

CHERYL
Oh, Dougie. Don't go getting all negative again.

DOUGIE
We've got to. I've got to.

CHERYL
No. It's not bad. If the doctors are talking about surgery that's good. That means there's hope. They wouldn't talk about surgery if there wasn't hope.

DOUGIE
You think so?

CHERYL
Yes. I know so.

DOUGIE
No. That's just what doctors do. They're like firemen. Firemen don't just stand around watching a house burn—they keep fighting the fire till there's nothing left.

CHERYL
Oh my God, don't be telling Dr. Azim he's like firemen.

DOUGIE
Anyway I'm not talking about that.
I wrote a letter.

CHERYL
Who are you writing letters to?

DOUGIE
It's there on the computer.

CHERYL
Is it to me?

DOUGIE
No. But you can read it. Just click on it there.

DOUGIE *heads outside.*

CHERYL
You're freaking me out a little bit, Dougie.

SANDY
Dad?

DOUGIE
You can both read the letter.

CHERYL goes to the computer. She sits and clicks on a document on the screen. SANDY sits beside her. They both read the letter on the screen.

Outside DOUGIE comes around the corner of the trailer. He sits on the ground with his back to the trailer. It feels as if he's been there before in times of distress. Like a child hiding behind the sofa.

CHERYL and SANDY continue to read. They grow horrified. SANDY doesn't need to read more. She moves to find her father.

CHERYL
Oh my God . . . Oh my God . . . Sandy . . . ?

SANDY
I know, Mom. I know.

CHERYL continues to read.

SANDY comes around the trailer searching for DOUGIE.

At a certain point CHERYL will close the laptop and sit on the sofa weeping.

Dad, get up off the ground.

DOUGIE
Why did you write me that poem?

SANDY
I knew you were sad.

DOUGIE
Did you know?

SANDY
No, Dad.

DOUGIE
It felt like you knew.

SANDY
I just knew you were sad.

DOUGIE
Say the poem for me? Would you?

SANDY
I don't know if I can, Dad.

> *DOUGIE offers SANDY the slim chapbook he has been clutching.*

DOUGIE
Once here was a village . . .
Once here was a village . . .

SANDY
Once here was a village some people had made.
Once here was a village
Once here were houses and a school and a place to go to die.
Now burnt to an ember.
An ember in the ash.
Warm. Like your heart.

Stand in the circle.
the circle we made and are made of.
Turn and see,
here is joy, here is sadness.
Points on the same line.

DOUGIE
(prompting) Fear not time . . .
Fear not time . . .

SANDY
Fear not Time.
Though it will chase us, always faster,
if we stop,
Time runs past us.
And without us to chase it will disappear.
Dissolve.
Less material than memory
Time will die.

DOUGIE
Time will die . . .

SANDY
Time will die and leave us finally alone together.
To be loved.
I carry you home.

DOUGIE
I carry you home . . .

SANDY
I carry you home,
now an ember in the ash.
Glowing goodness.
We will see now how simple,
how good
how true.

In a nearby by field fireworks go off. A big sound and a wonderful light.

I carry you with me.

DOUGIE
Yes.

DOUGIE and SANDY and CHERYL all look up into the colourful light.

Blackout.

End.

Daniel MacIvor is one of Canada's most accomplished playwrights and performers. Winner of the prestigious Elinore and Lou Siminovitch Prize, the GLAAD Award, the Governor General's Literary Award and many others, Daniel's plays have been met with acclaim throughout North America.

First edition: February 2021
Printed and bound in Canada by Rapido Books, Montreal

Jacket design by Leon Aureus
Author photo © Guntar Kravis

PLAYWRIGHTS
CANADA PRESS
202-269 Richmond St. W.
Toronto, ON
M5V 1X1
416.703.0013

info@playwrightscanada.com
www.playwrightscanada.com
@playcanpress